Our Kitchen

AN EXPERIENCE AMONG FAMILY—
COOKING, SONGS, HYMNS, AND POEMS

ALBA MERCEDES TAVAREZ

Copyright © 2022 Alba Mercedes Tavarez.

All rights reserved. No part of this book may be reproduced, stored, or transmitted by any means—whether auditory, graphic, mechanical, or electronic—without written permission of both publisher and author, except in the case of brief excerpts used in critical articles and reviews. Unauthorized reproduction of any part of this work is illegal and is punishable by law.

ISBN: 979-8-88640-292-6 (sc)
ISBN: 979-8-88640-293-3 (hc)
ISBN: 979-8-88640-294-0 (e)

Because of the dynamic nature of the Internet, any web addresses or links contained in this book may have changed since publication and may no longer be valid. The views expressed in this work are solely those of the author and do not necessarily reflect the views of the publisher, and the publisher hereby disclaims any responsibility for them.

One Galleria Blvd., Suite 1900, Metairie, LA 70001
1-888-421-2397

CONTENTS

Dedication v
Acknowledgments vii
Introduction ix

Recipes 1
    Chicken Fricassee 2
    Sofrito 3
    Pasteles de Masa 4
    Mashed Green Plantains 7
    Stewed Beans 8
    Rice with Pigeon Peas 9
    Beef Stew 11
    Sancocho 12
    Coconut Flan 15
    Pasteles de Yuca 16
    Green Banana Patties (Alcapurias) 19
    Coconut Bread Pudding 20
    Empanadas 21
    Ripe Plantain Meat Pie 22
    Shoulder Pork 24
    Sweet Rice 25
    Coconut Kisses 27

Food for the Soul 29
    The Greatest Grandmother Ever 30
    Mother's Day 31
    The Emigrant's Mother 32
    Only One Mother 33
    I Gave My Life for Thee 34
    Make Me a Blessing 36
    If I Could Help Somebody 37
    Stopping by the Woods About the
    Author on a Snowy Evening 38

About the Author 39

DEDICATION

This book is dedicated to my mother, Mercedes Pratts Andino. She had twelve children. They called us the twelve tribes of Mercedes. In our last family reunion, the photographer placed us by generations in order to take our photos. My mother was a great cook. She enjoyed preparing delicious meals for her family. To love is to give. She gave her life to her children.

ACKNOWLEDGMENTS

First, I must thank my sisters Abilia and Awilda. They provided the recipes that appeared in my first book, *Nuestra Cocina*.

To my daughters Aimee, Ivelisse, Lisa, and Tracey, my thanks for letting me use your kitchens.

My brother, Arnaldo, was kind enough to translate *Nuestra Cocina* to this book. My sincere gratitude.

Alina, my granddaughter, typed the first draft. Thanks!

Ivelisse formatted the final manuscript. Her help is greatly appreciated.

Director Enrique Rulof, pastor, professor, and writer, published my first book. I consider him my mentor. Thank you from the bottom of my heart. Your many books provides me with hours of good reading.

To my mother, Mercedes, thank you because when I was hungry, you gave me food to eat, and when I was thirsty you gave me to drink.

INTRODUCTION

I was twelve years old when my aunt Virginia began to talk to me about cooking. The apartment belonged to my aunt Felicita, but the kitchen belonged to my aunt Virginia. After inviting me, she spoke to me sweetly and affectionately and said to me, "If you come here after school, I will teach you how to cook." I loved being near her. So after school I visited my aunt, and she would teach me.

She would show me how to stew the beans and make rice. Later on, my mother also spoke to me about her cooking. "Come, Alba, taste this rice pudding and tell me if you like it. Is something missing? Is it too sweet or too salty? Perhaps it needs more coconut milk or sweet spices." One of my mother's greatest pleasures was cooking for her family. What a privilege it was for me that my mother considered my taste. That gesture made me feel loved by my mother.

My father also spoke to me while I was cooking. He had gastrointestinal problems. He could only eat bland foods such as boiled rice in milk and a mild custard we call maizena. "Alba," he would say to me, "be mindful that it does not turn out lumpy. I don't like to find lumps in the maizena." He was very demanding, but I knew that if he scraped the plate, he liked what I cooked.

Through the years I learned the importance of sharing the food with others. When I was a child, I remember vividly that my father shared the roasted pig at Christmas with the neighbors, and my mother shared her sweet rice. When my mother cooked, everyone was invited to eat; no one was excluded. "Either everyone eats or no one eats," she would say.

I cherish sweet memories of the coconut ice cream, the sweet rice-and-coconut pudding, and many other delights that I enjoyed as a young girl. That was how I developed my good taste in food.

My sister Abilia did not want anyone near her when she was cooking. If someone asked her for fried pork rind, she would say no. She would not share the fried pork rinds. She would eat them all herself.

My memories are kept in an imaginary trunk. In my memory trunk, I find one of my sisters, America. She was different. She loved to share her cooking. When she made her shrimp soup, she would call me and invite me to share the soup. My sister enjoyed eating meat. She would not only eat the meat; she would also eat the bones. She had strong teeth.

When I had my kitchen, I shared my cooking with friends and family. Those were the days. People would come to visit, and my aunt Virginia would make freshly brewed coffee. There was room for all at my table. Our house was called Hotel Tavarez because we had many guests.

My brother, Arnaldo, once spoke to me from his kitchen. He wanted to stew beans but did not know how. He asked me, and I explained to him how it was done. I spoke to him in his kitchen and shared what my aunt Virginia and my mother, Mercedes, had taught me.

My mother took great pride in her cooking. In those days, food spoke louder than words. I hear her gentle voice when I roast pork. I hear my father's strong voice saying, "This portion of the roasted pork is for our neighbors." When I savor a dish of delicious, sweet rice, I hear my mother asking me, "How is it? Do you like it?"

Today, I know that I never again will enjoy the sweet rice, coconut ice cream, and many other delicacies my mother used to cook. Never again will I savor the coconut pudding my aunt Virginia made. The kitchen of my mother is closed. The kitchen of my aunt Virginia is closed. Only they have the keys.

Recipes

CHICKEN FRICASSEE

Ingredients

chicken (3 pounds)
oil (¼ cup)
onion, large (1)
green pepper, medium (1)
garlic (3 cloves)
juice of one lemon
bay leaf, large (1)
salt (2 tablespoons)
cumin (¼ tablespoon)

saffron or paprika (¼ tablespoon)
black pepper, grated (¼ tablespoon)
water (2 ½ cups)
potatoes, cut into cubes (1 pound)
tomato sauce (8 ounces)
capers (¼ cup)
white wine (¼ cup)
green olives (¼ cup)
green peas (1 cup)

Procedure

- In a large skillet, sauté the chicken in oil.
- Add the onion, green pepper, and garlic.
- Cook until the greens are cooked.
- Add the lemon juice, bay leaf, salt, cumin, saffron, black pepper, and water.
- Cover and cook at medium heat for 20 minutes.
- Add the potatoes and cook until done.
- Remove the skin and the bones from the chicken, and cut the chicken into small cubes and sauté again.
- Add the tomato sauce, raisins, capers, wine, olives, and green peas.

Cook on low heat for 15 minutes. Serve hot. This makes 6 servings.

SOFRITO

Some of the recipes offered in this book include an ingredient referred to in Puerto Rico as sofrito. This is a mix of spices that generally include onions, green peppers, garlic, cilantro, and sweet chili peppers. These are diced thinly or combined in a blender in small or larger quantities that are refrigerated for future use. The typical mix for a regular dish of six portions would be as follows:

onion, small, diced thinly (1)
green pepper, small, diced thinly (1)
garlic, diced thinly (2 cloves)
sweet chili peppers, diced thinly (3)
cilantro leaves (1 tablespoon)

These ingredients, when mixed, are sautéd in a skillet or pot in a small amount of olive oil for about 5 minutes and combined with the other ingredients of the recipe. This mix lend that special flavor that is typical of Puerto Rican cooking. (This page may serve as reference whenever a recipe calls for sofrito.)

PASTELES DE MASA

Ingredients

- sofrito mix (as previously described)
- green bananas (6 pounds)
- green plantain (1)
- fresh pumpkin (2 ounces)
- yautias (3)
- salt (½ cup)
- pork shoulder meat, chopped (3 pounds)
- vegetable oil (¾ cups) mixed with achiote coloring (¼ cup)
- Sazón with achiote (2 packets)
- green olives with pimento filling (8 ounces)
- capers (1 ounces)
- raisins (8 ounces, optional)
- evaporated milk (14 ounces)
- water (2 cups)
- aluminum foil cut in 8–12 inch squares (60 squares)

This should be done just before preparing the pasteles to make sure you have the right size.

Procedure

- In a large pot pour sofrito and ¼ cup oil with achiote coloring. Cook for 5 minutes.
- Add the pork meat and cook for another 5 minutes, stirring at times.
- Add the 2 cups of water, cover the pot, and cook for another 10 minutes, stirring at times and making sure that the mixture does not dry.

- Remove pot from heat and set aside.
- Grate the bananas, plantain, yautias, and pumpkin. Mix these together in an over-sized pot.
- Add the salt and the liquid from the pot with the meat that was set aside, and mix thoroughly.
- Add the evaporated milk and mix thoroughly.
- In 3 separate bowls, place the ¾ cup of oil with achiote coloring in one, the cloves in another, and the capers (and raisins, which are optional) in the third.
- Place a sheet of aluminum foil on a flat surface, and with a teaspoon, smear a small portion of the oil with achiote in the middle of the sheet and spread in a circular motion to make the shape of an oval the size of the spoon used to pour the masa mixture.
- Add a large spoon of masa on the aluminum foil on top of the oval-sized oile and spread in an oval shape until about ⅓ inch thick.
- Place a tablespoon of the meat mix on the masa, add 2 olives, 2 capers, and 4 raisins (optional).
- Fold the sheet over the mix. Fold 2 more times (if, at this time, you do not have enough foil, you know you need a bigger piece of foil). Now roll up each side of the aluminum. Make sure that the folds and the edges are rolled to form a waterproof seal.
- Repeat the steps until the ingredients are used up.

Place desired number of pasteles in a pot of boiling water and cook for 45 minutes.

You have the option to freeze the pasteles. When cooking frozen pasteles, add salt to a pot of boiling water and cook for 1 ½ hours.

MASHED GREEN PLANTAINS

Ingredients

green plantain (1)
garlic (2 cloves)
pork rind or thick bacon (2 ounces)
olive oil (2 tablespoons plus ½ cup)
salt (1 teaspoon)

Procedure

- Peel and cut the plantain in small ½ inch slices. (Optional: season each slice with salt and pepper.)
- In a medium-sized skillet, heat the ½ cup of oil.
- Fry the plantain pieces.

Remove the plantain pieces from the oil, and place them on a paper towel.

- In a small-sized skillet, heat 2 tablespoons of oil.
- Cut the pork or bacon into small pieces and fry to a crisp.
- Save the skillet with the oil.
- Peel and mash the cloves of garlic in a mortar and pestle.
- Mash the plantain pieces, gradually adding the pork or bacon (with the oil in which they were fried) and the mashed garlic as the plantain is being mashed.

Form the mix into a ball or mound and serve by itself or with sauce of choice.

STEWED BEANS

Ingredients

beans (14 ounces)
potato, cut in cubes (1)
fresh pumpkin cut in cubes (1 two inch square)
onion, small, diced (1)
water (1 ½ cups)
cilantro leaves (1 tablespoon)
garlic, diced (1 clove)
Sazón (1 packet)
olive oil (2 tablespoons)
tomato sauce (4 ounces)

Procedure

- In a medium-sized pot over medium heat, pour in the olive oil.
- Add the onion, green pepper, garlic and cilantro leaves, sauté for 5 minutes.
- Add the Sazón, potatoes and the pumpkin, and sauté for 3 minutes.
- Add the water, tomato sauce, and beans.
- Boil until the liquid thickens.
- Serve with rice.

RICE WITH PIGEON PEAS

Ingredients

    sofrito mix (described in earlier recipes)
    rice (2 cups)
    pigeon peas (14 ounces)
    Sazón with achiote (1 packet)
    chorizo, diced (2 ounces)
    olive oil (2 tablespoons)
    tomato sauce (2 tablespoons)
    water (2 cups)

Procedure

- In a medium-sized pot over medium heat, heat the olive oil.
- Add the sofrito, Sazón with achiote, chorizo, and tomato sauce.
- Sauté for about 5 minutes. Add the water, rice, and pigeon peas.
- Mix the ingredients, and let them boil gen-tly until the liquid evaporates.
- Cover the pot, lower the heat, and allow the rice to cook for another 30 minutes. No need to stir.

BEEF STEW

Ingredients

beef sirloin or chuck (2 pounds)
potatoes, large, cut in cubes (2)
tomato sauce (4 ounces)
Sazón with achiote (1 packet)
olives with pimento filling (½ cup)
capers (1 tablespoon)
salt (1 tablespoon)
water (2 cups)
olive oil (2 tablespoons)
sofrito mix (see reference page)

Procedure

- In a large pot, heat the olive oil over medium heat, add the sofrito, and cook for 4 min-utes, stirring occasionally.
- Cut the beef into cubes, add them into the pot, and cook until the meat turns brown. Add the water, olives, capers, and potatoes.
- Cover the pot and continue cooking at medium heat until the meat becomes tender. Add the tomato sauce and Sazón with achiote.
- Uncover the pot and continue to cook until the liquid is reduced to a thick sauce.

Serve with rice.

SANCOCHO

Ingredients

pork shoulder meat, cut in medium cubes (2 pounds)
pork bones, if available (1 pound)
green plantain (1)
yautias, peeled and cut in small pieces (½ pound)
fresh pumpkin, peeled and cut in small pieces (½ pound)
malanga, peeled and cut in medium cubes (1 pound)
celery root (apio), peeled and cut in small cubes (1 pound)
green bananas, peeled and cut in half (4)
ñame, peeled and cut in medium cubes (1 pound)
Sazón with achiote (1 packet)
salt (2 tablespoons)
olive oil (2 tablespoons)
tomato sauce (6 ounces)
water, enough to cover all the ingredients sofrito mix

Procedure

- Peel and grate the green plantains. Place it on cheesecloth, and squeeze the liquid out.
- Mix a little oil and salt with the plantains and set aside.
- In a large skillet over medium heat, heat the olive oil.
- Add pork until it browns.
- Add the sofrito. Cook for another 4 minutes and set aside.
- In an oversized pot, place the yautia, pump-kin, malanga, celery root, green bananas, and ñame. Pour enough water to cover all ingredients completely. Heat on high and bring to boil.

- Add the salt, tomato sauce, and Sazón, then stir well.
- Add the bones and the contents of the skillet that was set aside.
- Cover the pot, lower the heat, and continue to cook for 20 minutes.
- Add the plantains that were set aside, and continue to cook until the liquid thickens into a sauce.

Serve hot.

COCONUT FLAN

Ingredients

eggs, large (6)
coconut milk (14 ounces)
condensed milk (14 ounces)
Coco Lopez (14 ounces)

vanilla extract (1 tablespoon)
Puerto Rican rum (1 tablespoon)
sugar, for the caramel (1 cup)
Preheat oven 350 degrees.

Procedure

- In a small pot, prepare the caramel by heat-ing the sugar at medium heat, stirring until it melts and turns dark brown.
- Pour the caramel evenly into the bottom of a baking mold 9 inches in diameter and 4 inches deep. Set this aside.
- In a large bowl, whisk the eggs until the whites and the yolks are thoroughly mixed.
- Add the condensed milk, and whisk to combine add the Coco Lopez and whisk to combine.
- Add the coconut milk and whisk to combine.
- Add the vanilla extract and whisk.
- Add the Puerto Rican rum, and continue to whisk.
- Pour the mix into the caramelized baking mold.
- Place the baking mold into a larger baking pan that is half-filled with warm water. Place the tray in the oven.
- Bake the flan for 60 minutes, but test with a toothpick to make sure it is fully baked before removing from oven.

Allow the flan to cool before refrigerating.

Refrigerate for at least 4 hours before serving.

PASTELES DE YUCA

Ingredients

yucca (8 pounds)
pork shoulder meat, cut in small cubes (2 pounds)
sofrito mixture
raisins (¼ pound) (optional)
olives stuffed with pimento (6 ounces)
olive oil (2 tablespoons plus ¾ cup)
achiote seeds (3 tablespoons)
salt (2 tablespoons plus 1 tablespoon)
Sazón packet (1)
evaporated milk (14 ounces)
sugar (1 teaspoon)
water (2 cups)
aluminum foil 8–12 inch squares (60)

This should be done just before preparing the pasteles to make sure you have the right size.

Procedure

- Peel the yucca with a dull dinner knife. Grate them and remove the liquid by squeezing in cheesecloth. Place in a medium-sized pot and set aside.
- In a separate medium-sized pot, pour the 2 tablespoons of olive oil and heat. Add the cubes of pork and cook until brown.
- Add the sofrito and the Sazón, stir lightly, lower the heat, and cook for another 8 minutes.
- Add the 2 cups of water and cover the pot.
- Reduce the heat and cook until liquid becomes a light sauce.
- Remove from the stove and set aside.
- In a small skillet heat the ¾ cup of oil at medium heat, add the achiote seeds, and stir until the oil turns red.

- Remove from the stove.
- Strain into a bowl to separate the oil from the seeds. Discard the seeds, and divide the oil into two equal parts.
- Take the pot with the grated yucca, and add it to just the sauce from the meat mix. Add one part of the oil with achiote, 2 tablespoons of salt, a teaspoon of sugar, and the evaporated milk.
- Mix everything thoroughly. It should produce a pasty mix.
- In three separate bowls, place the raisins in one, the olives in another, and the other part of the oil with achiote in the third.
- Place a sheet of aluminum foil on a flat surface, and with a teaspoon, smear a small portion of the oil with achiote in the middle of the sheet and spread in a circular motion to make the shape of an oval the size of the spoon used to pour the yucca mixture.
- Add a large spoon of yucca mixture on the aluminum foil on top of the oval-sized oil, and spread in an oval shape until about ⅓ inch thick.
- Place a tablespoon of the meat mix on the yucca, add 2 olives, 2 capers, and 4 raisins (optional)
- Fold the sheet over the mix. Fold 2 more times (if at this time you do not have enough foil, you know you need a bigger piece of foil). Now roll up each side of the aluminum. Make sure that the folds and the edges are rolled to form a waterproof seal.
- Repeat the steps until the ingredients are used up.

Place desired number of pasteles in a pot of boiling water and cook for 45 minutes.

You have the option to freeze the pasteles. When cooking frozen pasteles, add salt to a pot of boiling water and cook for 1 ½ hours.

GREEN BANANA PATTIES (ALCAPURIAS)

Ingredients

green bananas (6)
pork shoulder meat, diced (1 pound)
green olives stuffed with pimento (½ cup)
olive oil (1 tablespoon)
vegetable oil (enough for frying the patties desired)
salt (1 teaspoon)
water (2cups)
sofrito mix

Procedure

- In a medium-sized pot, boil the water, salt, and the meat. Cook for 15 minutes.
- In a small skillet, heat the olives, add the sofrito, and cook for 4 minutes, stirring occasionally.
- Add sofrito mix to the meat, stir, and cover the pot. Cook until the liquid thickens.
- Peel the bananas, grate them, and squeeze out the liquid using cheesecloth.
- Mix ⅔ of the liquid from the cooked meat with the bananas and combine to a pasty consistency.
- In a large skillet, heat the vegetable oil for frying.
- In a small flat plate, with a large spoon, place an amount of the banana mix on top of the meat, creating a pattie.
- Slide the pattie into the hot oil and fry on both sides.

Serve hot.

COCONUT BREAD PUDDING

Ingredients

French bread, plain (1 pound)
butter (2 ounces)
eggs (2)
dry coconut (1)
milk (1 ¼ cups)
sugar (1 ½ cups plus ½ cup)
salt (1 teaspoons)
ground cinnamon (½ teaspoon)
cloves (½ teaspoon)
evaporated milk (1 cup)
raisins (1 cup)

Preheat oven to 350 degrees.

Procedure

- In a medium skillet, at low heat, melt ½ cup sugar, stir occasionally until liquid and dark brown (caramel).
- Pour the caramel into a round baking mold 1 inches in diameter and 3 inches deep-set a side.
- Soak the bread in the milk in a large bowl until bread is soft. Remove the bread from the milk, and shred it.
- Add the butter to the soaked bread.
- Add the eggs, and mix them in one at a time.
- Grate the coconut, add the 1 ¼ cups of water, and squeeze well in a linen cloth to extract the coconut milk.
- Add the coconut milk to the bread mix, fold, and add the 1 ½ cups of sugar, salt, cinnamon, cloves, and evaporated milk. Mix everything well.
- Pour the mix into the caramelized baking mold. Place the baking mold into a baking pan half-filled with warm water.
- Place the baking pan in oven, and bake for 1 hour. When it is done, remove from oven.
- Remove from water, and allow to cool to room temperature. It may also be refrigerated.

EMPANADAS

Ingredients

chopped meat (1 pound)
onion, small, minced (1)
green pepper, small, minced (1)
garlic, minced (4 cloves)
adobo (1 tablespoon)
Sazón (1 packet)
tomato sauce (8 ounces)
Colby shredded cheese (2 cups)
pie crust (1 box containing 3 rolls)
Preheat oven to 400 degrees.

Procedure

- In a large skillet at medium heat, cook the meat until brown, add the onions, peppers, garlic, adobo, Sazón, and tomato sauce.
- Mix thoroughly and continue to cook for 15 minutes.
- Unroll the pie crust and cut it in round sections 3 inches in diameter (should yield 25 in number).
- Brush the edges of each pie crust section with water as they become ready to be filled with the meat.
- Place one tablespoon of the meat mix at the center of the pie crust section, sprinkle with cheese, fold in half, and seal the edges by pressing them with a fork.
- Place the sections in a baking pan greased with butter, and bake for 15 minutes.
- Remove from oven.

Serve hot.

RIPE PLANTAIN MEAT PIE

Ingredients

plantains, ripe (6)
ground beef (1 pound)
garlic, minced (4 cloves)
onion, minced (1)
green pepper, minced (1)
adobo (2 teaspoons)
Sazón (1 packet)
oregano, ground (2 tablespoons)
green olives filled with pimento (½ cup)
tomato sauce (8 ounces)
Colby cheese (2 cups)
eggs, whisked (6)
milk (¼ cup)
coconut or vegetable oil (enough to fry the plantains)
Preheat oven to 350 degrees.

Procedure

- Peel and cut the plantains into thin, rectan-gular slices, about 3 inches in length.
- In a large skillet, on medium heat, heat the oil and fry the plantain slices until tender, turning them over once.
- Remove plantains from skillet and place them on paper towels.
- In another skillet, brown the ground beef, add the garlic, onions, green peppers and tomato sauce.

- Cook over medium heat for 10 minutes, add the adobo, Sazón, oregano and olives, simmer another 20 minutes.
- Remove from heat.
- Grease a 9 by 13 inch baking pan with the oil left from frying the plantains.
- Place half of the plantain slices in a single layer in the casserole dish, top them with half of the meat mix, sprinkle one cup of the cheese over the meat. Repeat these steps with remaining plantain slices, meat, and cheese.
- Add milk to whisked eggs, mix, then pour the mixture over the contents in the casserole. Place the casserole in the oven and bake for 30 minutes.

Serve hot.

SHOULDER PORK

Ingredients

shoulder pork, whole (10 pounds)
garlic (1 full head, each clove mashed well)
ground black pepper (1 tablespoon)
salt (2 tablespoons)
Preheat oven to 350 degrees.

Procedure

- In a mortar and pestle, mash the garlic cloves. Combine them with the salt and pepper, preparing a mix to rub on the pork shoulder.
- Wash the pork with white vinegar, then dry it with paper towels. Rub the meat thoroughly with the garlic mix (make sure you use all the mix), and place it in a roasting pan.
- Cover the pan with aluminum foil and place the pan with the meat in the oven. Roast for 3 hours.
- Remove the aluminum foil, raise the heat to 375 degrees and continue roasting for another 1 hour or until the outer rind of the meat becomes crispy, then remove from oven.

Serve hot.

SWEET RICE

Ingredients

short or medium grain rice (1 cup)
coconut milk (1 can)
Coco Lopez (1 can)
condensed milk (1 can)
cinnamon sticks (5)
cloves (2 tablespoons)
fresh ginger, minced (4 ounces)
butter (¼ pound)
salt (1 tablespoon)
ground cinnamon (½ teaspoon)
raisins (⅓ cup)
water (6 cups)

Procedure

- In a large pot, boil 6 cups of water, the cinnamon sticks, the cloves, and the ginger. Lower the heat and simmer for 20 minutes. Remove from heat.
- Strain the water into another large pot. Discard the cinnamon sticks, cloves, and ginger.
- Add butter, salt, and coconut milk to the water, and continue boiling.
- Rinse the rice and add it to the pot. Lower the heat, and simmer for another 15 minutes, stirring frequently.
- Add the Coco Lopez, condensed milk, and raisins. Cook for another 15 minutes.
- Pour into a deep dish. Sprinkle the top with ground cinnamon.

Serve hot or cold.

COCONUT KISSES

Ingredients

wheat flour (½ cup)
salt (⅛ teaspoon)
coconut, shredded (2 ½ cups)
milk (⅔ cups)
vanilla extract (1 teaspoon)
Preheat oven to 350 degrees.

Procedure

- Grease a cookie sheet with butter.
- In a large bowl, sift the flour and salt.
- Stir in the coconut.
- Add the condensed milk and the vanilla extract, and stir thoroughly to make a batter.
- Drop teaspoons of batter one inch apart on the cookie sheet.
- Place in oven, and bake for 20 minutes or until golden brown.

Remove from the oven and let cool.

Food for the Soul

THE GREATEST GRANDMOTHER EVER

(by Alina Tavarez, fifteen years old)

I love you so much
We have been together
Ever since I was born
Now that you are an hour

And fifteen minutes away
It is hard for me
Missing you and all.
I have always loved you

And I always will
I do not know what
I would do without you.

I remember you reading to me
Helping me learn to tie my shoes
Cooking farina for me
Taking me to bingo when I was three

I remember everything.
I miss you so
I want you to know
You are the greatest grandmother ever.

MOTHER'S DAY

(by Ivelisse Tavarez, nine years old)

It's not only on Mother's Day
That Mother likes a special smile
Though we celebrate it in May
It's not only on Mother's Day

She likes the special things we say to her
She likes them all the time!
It's not only on Mother's Day
That Mother likes a special smile!

THE EMIGRANT'S MOTHER

In a small seaport in the south of Spain, in a cottage close to the sea, lived an old woman who was always sad while her eyes searched the vastness of the sea. She was a poor widow who had a son who, when he found himself strong enough to work, crossed the sea with hopes to become rich, saying to his mother that he would not forget her.

Months went by, years went by, and a letter arrived—a short, emotionless, and cold letter that denoted the platitudes of a miserable man who had forgotten the love of his mother.

His poor mother would blame his workload, and after months and then another year neglected by her ungrateful son, she would say as if speaking to him, "Why don't you write to your sad and crying mother? Why don't you cheer me with words of love? Don't you know, your last letter brought no comfort or sacred joy that nowhere I can find? Oh! If you knew the sufferings that plague me or understood the concept of 'motherhood,' you would write your mother a letter to calm all my fears and pain. Write me again, my jewel, I forgive you. I do not ask for money. No, my son. Speak to me of your triumphs or your failures so that my sleepless nights will turn to peace."

The gentle breeze carried abroad the message. It reached a very ugly place and found the ungrateful son in all his vices rejecting still his mother's tender love.

Upon that scene, the gentle breeze turned somber. It took up form and glistened like a knife, as if to pierce the chest of that villain who did not appreciate what a beast would now adore.

Perhaps the breeze told the old woman all, and when she went to the beach one day in a delirium, she kissed the son she adored, and at that time, the portals of eternity were opened to her.

ONLY ONE MOTHER

(A gift from Lisa Tavarez)

Hundreds of stars in the pretty sky,
Hundreds of shells on the shore together
Hundreds of birds that go singing by,
Hundreds of lambs in the sunny weather,

Hundreds of dewdrops to greet the dawn
Hundreds of bees in the purple clover,
Hundreds of butterflies on the lawn,
But only one mother,
The wide world over.

I GAVE MY LIFE FOR THEE

(Hymns of Faith and Praise 12)

I gave my life for thee; my precious blood I shed, that thou might ransomed be, and quickened from the dead. I gave, I gave my life for thee. What hast thou given for me? I gave, I gave my life for thee. What hast thou given for me?

My father's house of light; my splendor my throne, I left for earthly night, for wanderings sad and alone. I left, I left it all for thee. What have you left for me? I left, I left it all for thee. What have you left for me?

I suffered much for thee, more than thy tongue can tell. Of bitterest agony, to rescue thee from hell. I've borne, I've borne it all for thee. What hast thou borne for me? I've borne, I've borne it all for thee. What hast thou borne for me?

And I have brought to thee, down from my home above, salvation full and free, my pardon and my love. I bring, I bring rich gifts to thee. What do you bring for me? I bring, I bring rich gifts to thee. What do you bring for me?

Sing them over again to me, wonderful words of life; let me more of their beauty see, wonderful words of life. Words of life and beauty, teach me faith and duty.

Beautiful words, wonderful words, wonderful words of life. Beautiful words, wonderful words, wonder-ful words of life.

Christ, the blessed one gives to all, wonderful words of life. Sinner list to the loving call, wonderful words of life. All so freely given, wooing us to heaven – Sweetly echo the gospel call, wonderful words of life; offer pardon and peace to all, wonderful words of life. Jesus only savior, sanctify forever

MAKE ME A BLESSING

(Hymn of the Christian Life 255)

Out in the highways and byways of life
Many are weary and sad
Carry the sunshine where darkness is rife
Making the sorrowing glad

Chorus

Make me a blessing
Make me a blessing
Out of my life may Jesus shine
Make me a blessing
Oh Savior I pray
Make me a blessing
To someone today

Tell the sweet story of Christ and his love
Tell of his power to forgive
Others will trust him if only you prove true
Every moment you live

Give as it was given to you in your need
Love as the Master loved you
Be to the helpless a helper indeed
Unto your mission be true.

IF I COULD HELP SOMEBODY

(Spiritual Song)

If I could help somebody as I pass along
If I could help somebody with a word or song
If I could help somebody that is doing wrong
Then my living shall not be in vain

No, my living shall not be in vain
No, my living shall not be in vain
If I can help somebody as I pass along
Then my living shall not be in vain

STOPPING BY THE WOODS ABOUT THE AUTHOR ON A SNOWY EVENING

Robert Frost

Whose woods these are I think I know.
His house is in the village, though.
He will not see me stopping here.
To watch his woods fill up with snow.
My little horse must think it queer
To stop without a farmhouse near
Between the woods and frozen lake
The darkest evening of the year.
He gives his harness bells a shake
To ask if there is some mistake.
The only other sound's the sweep
Of easy wind and downy flake.
The woods are lovely, dark, and deep,
But I have promises to keep,
And miles to go before I sleep…
And miles to go before I sleep…

ABOUT THE AUTHOR

Alba Mercedes Tavarez was born in Coamo, Puerto Rico. At the age of twelve, her parents moved the family to New York. She graduated from Andrew Jackson High School and received her BA in Spanish from New Paltz College. She completed some work in the Masters of Educational Psychology at Marist College in Poughkeepsie, New York.

She worked for the US Army Corps of Engineers as a clerk-stenographer, for the US Military Academy at West Point, New York, and as a secretary to the civilian personnel officer. She also worked as a customs aide at the Houston Intercontinental Airport in Texas. Back in New York, she worked for Vocational and Educational Services for Individuals with Disabilities (VESID), as a counselor assistant.

Robert Redford once said, "Service is the rent that we pay for living. Life is not free. We need to pay for living. There are various ways for paying; the most rewarding in my view, is service."

We are born to serve. We serve our children, we serve our communities, we serve God, we serve the needy, and we serve ourselves. Yes, "service is the rent we pay for living."